A Method for the Madness:
An Introduction to Qualitative
Futures Squares

Adair Daniels

To my wife Mariah, your love and support
have allowed me to become the man I am today.

Table of Contents

Chapter 1: Introduction

Predicting the future accurately is incredibly difficult. The future is always changing, and there are an infinite number of possibilities. However, this does not mean that we can't make meaningful predictions. One of the best ways to understand what may happen is to examine what has already happened. If I throw a ball at a wall nine times, and nine times it bounces back to me, I can predict that it's likely to bounce back to me the tenth time, that's pretty easy.

If I put some qualifiers on that, however, it becomes more accurate. If I throw the ball at the wall at a different angle, it's not as likely to bounce back to me. If I throw it much harder than I did the first nine times, I may wish to duck out of the way. So, to qualify the throw, I may wish to say that if I throw it a tenth time at the same angle and with the same amount of force, it's very likely to come back to me.

Meaningful futures predictions are enormously more difficult than the ball example, and the data isn't so nice and simple. However, qualifiers are still incredibly useful in formulating predictions. Even so, examining large industries or movements over a large period of time is far too complex to boil down to single outcomes such as in the ball example. When examining the future, it's instrumental to examine many outcomes.

The first step in examining possible outcomes is to develop a futures hypothesis. Just like a normal scientific hypothesis, a futures hypothesis is both an educated guess and a stepping stone to further investigation. Unlike a traditional scientific hypothesis, a futures hypothesis should by necessity account for multiple possible outcomes. While this drives a further level of integrity in the work, it certainly makes an already difficult task even harder. So, how can we make this easier? As you are reading an introduction to Qualitative Futures Squares, you do rightly already know my answer. However, let's explore how this would go without the QFS.

Let's say that I want to understand how the potential technology of asteroid mining may evolve. This is an example that we'll fully examine further in this book with the Qualitative Futures Square, but let's give it a go now. First, I need to figure out a timeframe that I'm interested in. Ten years? Twenty years? Let's go with twenty five years, for now. If I think of how technology is apt to progress in the next twenty five years, I can see a reasonable, potential future where humans have begun mining asteroids in twenty five years. Robotic swarm technology is one possible form of technology not proven in this arena that could be incredibly useful. Robotic swarm technology can allow very large numbers of very small robots to work in conjunction for a given goal, like mining an asteroid. Yet, would this technology be absolutely necessary for mining an asteroid? I don't think so, and neither do most companies salivating over the opportunities in asteroid mining. Helpful, but not necessary.

Should we close the book right there and consider the issue closed? Absolutely not. While it's feasible for us to be technologically capable of mining asteroids in twenty five years, that's not the only obstacle for such a future to arise. What about the legal aspect? As of right now, the United States is the only country in the world with space capabilities that has passed legislative support for corporations owning resources obtained in space. The legislation is tentative, and may be overturned. It also may be that it becomes a model for future legislation in other countries. It also may be that the situation sits in its exact position for the next twenty five years.

This legislative hurdle is very important, and the three paths leading forward from it are irreconcilable. So, how do we deal with it? Do we simply pick a favorite, either what we deem as most probable or most preferred? Yes, and no. Instead of picking a single path to analyze going forward, the most useful thing to do is to analyze each path separately, as an independently evolving possible future. If we handle it this way, we have no obligation to take a stance as to what is likely to happen yet. By independently investigating each potential future, we can maintain our intellectual honesty *as well as* our inherent bias (which absolutely everyone has) – and perhaps more importantly forego making poor attempts at answering questions that are outside of our expertise (as legislation is for me).

Looking forward in a future where this legislation becomes a model for legislation elsewhere, we can see how a future of asteroid mining evolves quite nicely. Even if a US-based company weren't to take to the stars and mine asteroids, someone else probably will. It's the nature of competition and disruption that an open path untried will be tried. If instead, the legislative situation remains as set, it's not quite such a foregone conclusion that asteroid mining will arise, at least within this timeframe. With only one capable country with legislative support, the situation is tentative internationally.

Will other countries accept materials mined by a US-based company in outer space? Such an open question comes with a measure of risk for business-minded individuals. This risk is not insurmountable, but considerable. So, let's investigate further. In this situation, it's highly unlikely NASA will get involved in asteroid mining. Without international support, an official government entity mining may seem arrogant, or even hostile. Whom does this leave as a possibility? In a risky, but technically justifiable situation, companies like SpaceX, Blue Origin, and Planetary Resources are strong possibilities for continuing the effort of asteroid mining. Whether or not these are the companies that choose to make the leap, the probability could be seen to lean in favor of someone making the attempt at asteroid mining even with this legislative outcome. This path also accounts for the possibility of the United States overturning the current legislation, but another country rising to take its place.

If, on the other hand, the outcome is that the United States legislation is overturned, and other countries do not legislate alternative pathways to legal asteroid mining, the situation is rather bleak. Looking forward along this path, the likelihood is diminutive that asteroid mining emerges as an industry within the next twenty five years. There are other possible hurdles to examine as well, but this is sufficient for now. We'll further develop forming futures hypotheses later.

Now, looking at our predictions, we have a startling conclusion: without having to make a decision on legislative likelihoods, 0we've discovered that the future seems to favor asteroid mining within twenty five years! As a matter of technology, the future holds no large obstacles.

As a legal matter, two out of three examined paths forward lend themselves to asteroid mining within twenty five years. Now this is useful!

Chapter 2: Futures Hypotheses

A futures hypothesis serves the same function as a scientific hypothesis – it provides a concise way to deliver a prediction about the results of the coming work. A futures hypothesis is not to be confused with the prediction itself, which often takes the form of a white paper. The hypothesis is an analysis of a situation prior to commencing actual research. Just as in standard scientific research, a structured hypothesis can streamline the necessary research to reach the desired ends. To understand why it's so important to have a structured futures hypothesis, let's first take a look at the field of futurism.

Futurism, or futures studies (and sometimes futurology), is an informal field. While multiple professional organizations of futurists do exist, such as the World Future Society, the Association of Professional Futurists, and the Millennium Project, there are no formal requirements for someone to call themselves a futurist. As such, there's any number of charlatans, soothsayers, and scammers that utilize the name of "futurist" to lend themselves credibility. So, how can you tell the fakes from serious futurists?

Serious futures studies *is* actually a scientific discipline, and as such is subject to the same (and perhaps greater) rigors as other scientific fields. A futurist should not just be capable of making a prediction, but justifying how he/she came to that conclusion. When I made the prediction in 2010 that the next Xbox system from Microsoft would be capable of streaming to a Windows PC, I was utilizing information from a multitude of areas, such as the trend of rising usage of streaming technology, the building trend of interconnected devices, and the business advantage Microsoft has with its market share of Windows personal computers. While this was a justifiable (and indeed a correct) prediction, it very well could have been false – and at the time, this was something I fully admitted.

Which brings us to the second differentiation of serious futurists – the acknowledgement of alternate futures. While it would be "wishy washy" in other fields, professional futurists need to utilize conditional words like "may", "should", "could", "likely", "probably", and "possibly". This is a form of intellectual honesty – no matter how keen our minds, no matter how accurate our tools, we can't completely reduce the universe to clockwork. In addition, it's extremely important to explore multiple paths from a stance of preparation.

The best way to ensure that these two indicators are clear to the reader is to include them from the beginning of a piece of work. As futurists, the onus is on us to ensure that these indicators are addressed inside the futures hypothesis of a work. To address the first indicator, a clear and concise explanation of factors considered should be included. To address the second indicator, there are a few approaches. One of them is how we handled asteroid mining above – by discussing the possible futures and what differentiates them. While this is sufficient to communicate the necessary information, it's hardly efficient. Another method, is of course, the Qualitative Futures Square. This is the purpose for which it was formulated.

Chapter 3: The Qualitative Futures Square

Title	Poor	Possible	Probable	Preferred
Short Range (<5 years)				
Middle Range (5-20 years)				
Long Range (20-50 years)				
Beyond (50-100 years)				

The Qualitative Futures Square (QFS) is a method of formulating a futures hypothesis, a tool that I developed for my own usage. Aside from addressing intellectual honesty, understanding multiple possible futures is *useful.* While it may be painful to do so, you can multiply your effectiveness (not only in futurism, but in everything) by simply admitting that you may be getting something wrong. Exploring multiple futures allows a consulting futurist to become far more useful than exploring a single possible future, by providing a means for the client to be prepared if circumstances change.

Embodying this, the QFS is a flexible tool, capable of being the first stepping stone in analyzing futures for industries, technologies, and events. As a tool for formulating hypotheses, it is appropriate that the input for the squares are guesses. It is, at its foundation, simply a tool for orderly stating what you believe will/may happen. It is equally useful for the reader as it is for the futurist. Following the structure of the QFS allows a futurist to easily segment their work in a standard, yet flexible way.

The axes of a QFS are "Order" (Poor, Possible, Probable, and Preferred) and "Timeline" (Short Range, Middle Range, and Long Range). As bias is impossible to remove entirely from futures studies, Preferred is filled first for Order, but comes last. Preferred allows the futurist to clearly state what they wish to happen. This allows the futurist to separate out their emotional bias and allows the reader to watch for wishful thinking. Probable is filled next, as this allows the futurist to clearly state their belief as to what will happen. This is another form of bias, the logical bias. While this may seem to be an odd thing to consider a bias, different futurists (and people in general) have different patterns in their thinking, allowing two people to state two different outcomes as the likely outcome from the same event. Next filled out is Possible, which allows the futurist to state what may happen, after removing what they want to happen and what they believe will happen. Poor is filled out last, and comes first, as it demonstrates the outcome the futurist wishes to avoid. Input from the Poor and Preferred boxes should at least partially overlap input in either the Probable or Possible boxes.

The Timeline definitions are actually flexible, though the ranges given are the most commonly useful. Even when using the standard <5, 5-20, 20-50, and 50-100 year ranges, it is still best to label the ranges you use. As a general rule of thumb, there should be a clear gradient of specificity from Short Range to Beyond, with Beyond making general speculations. There is a fine line between being general and being vague, and you should always guard against being unnecessarily vague. The exception to this rule has to do with Short Range and Middle Range, with Middle Range sometimes able to be a tad more specific than Short Range (as five years isn't all that much time to change from the current situation).

A QFS in a document should contain enough detail to fill about a page in a word processor. As a tool, it should be considered a philosophical/functional cousin to an outline, and has no need to contain detailed explanations or justification. A reader should be able to scan a QFS and gain a clear understanding about the direction of research in a paper, as well as the expectations of the futurist that wrote that paper. After the square proper, a short discussion of latchkey issues, synergistic developments, key players and wildcards should be included.

Latchkey issues are those that are make or break for a given QFS. As you may expect from our earlier exploration, legislation is a latchkey issue for asteroid mining. Synergistic developments are achievements in outside, but related industries that could prove quite useful for the technology/industry/event that you are exploring with the square. These aren't as important as latchkey issues, but are nevertheless important to keep an eye on. Robotic swarm technology, as discussed earlier in the book, is a synergistic development for asteroid mining.

Key players are companies, governments, government agencies, NGOs, and even individuals that have the likely potential to change the landscape of the object of the QFS. If they're influential enough to be included in the QFS, they should be explored separately in the key players section. Wildcards are events that have the same potential as key players to change the outcome of a QFS, but have a very low likelihood (general rule of thumb being estimated at <15%), or have a likelihood that's very difficult to predict (an example will come later in the book). However, there's no need to include extremely low likelihood (<1%) events, as then every wildcard section would have to include a number of apocalyptic scenarios that while may certainly have the potential to change the landscape of a QFS, aren't likely enough to generally consider seriously.

Having explored asteroid mining in the beginning, it's most fitting to explore asteroid mining once again utilizing the Qualitative Futures Square.

Asteroid Mining	Poor	Possible	Probable	Preferred
Short Range (<5 years)	Neither rocket recovery nor robot swarm technology may improve. Legislation may restrict space mining preemptively.	SpaceX may not make commercially useful progress on rocket recovery.	SpaceX may make large progress on rocket recovery, and robot swarm technology may continue to improve.	SpaceX may master rocket recovery, and robot swarm technology will continue to improve.
Middle Range (5-20 years)	Private companies may not make much of an effort to expand space tourism.	Private companies may attempt to expand space tourism, though fail at making a meaningful increase. Orbital hotels may simply have more advanced conceptual plans.	Private companies may expand operations in space tourism, with decent success. The first prototype orbital hotel may be deployed, though not initially inhabited. Robot swarm technology may see first usage in space.	Private companies may expand operations in space tourism and have functional orbital hotels. Robot swarm technology may see first usage in space. Space mining legislation may expand into more countries.
Long Range (20-50 years)	Asteroid mining may hit a stumbling block in the conceptual phase that reduces the chances of it becoming a reality.	Asteroid mining may still be in the conceptual phase.	Near-Earth asteroids may begin to be mined by smaller, rover like drones.	Robot swarm technology may be put to use in effectively mining asteroids. Asteroid mined materials begin to change the resource economy.
Beyond (50-100 years)	Asteroid mining may have been demonstrated to not be a feasible industry.	Asteroid mining may become a small effort to obtain rare metals.	Asteroid mining may prove to be a successful industry.	Asteroid mining may prove to be a successful industry and may replace Earth-based mining.

Latchkey issues: Legislation is a key issue for asteroid mining. As profitable of an enterprise as it is capable of being, the likelihood is diminishingly small that a company will seek to begin asteroid mining without legislative support. Investment levels are also crucial for asteroid mining. Both research & development and execution are going to be incredibly costly for asteroid mining, and the likelihood is low that governments will be willing to put forth that initial investment for some time.

Synergies: Robotic swarm technology is crucial for further down the road, and important progress must be made now. Asteroid mining can't be undertaken utilizing standard methods of mining on Earth, and robotic swarms present the most efficient way to mine asteroids. However, there are other possible methods, and so robotic swarm technology isn't quite a latchkey issue. Both space tourism and space hotels are heavily synergistic in a financial sense with asteroid mining. Space tourism and hotels can drive the heavy interest in space that will be necessary to handle the latchkey issue of investment. In turn, if/when asteroid mining is a standardized practice, it will further legitimize space-based enterprises, making investment into space tourism/hotel startups more appetizing for investors.

Key players: SpaceX is currently leading the charge for privatized space exploration. As such, it is likely that they will continue to do so. The United States is currently the only nation in the world with legislation authorizing space mining, and as such is likely to be host to whatever company decides to pursue asteroid mining. Planetary Resources is the company perhaps most likely to begin asteroid mining first, with plans to begin with near-Earth asteroids within the next decade or two. The robotics industry as a whole will play a key part with swarm robotics, though there will need to be (at least) one company specializing in the design of asteroid mining robotics, as the physics is drastically different.

Wildcards: The main possible wildcard is a government agency obtaining the funding to aggressively pursue asteroid mining. The likelihood for this is rather low (I estimate ~7%), but not so small as to ignore. Aggressive government pursuit would likely take the form of establishing the foundation for private industry to thrive from, and would radically speed up the above time schedule and lean outcomes toward Preferred.

This lays a perfect foundation to begin research from. In fact, this very foundation was used for my chapter "Astro-mining for Abundancy" in A Very Human Future, a book hitting the shelves soon. By following the structure laid out for the QFS, every avenue of research has a starting point. While I have larger personal knowledge of asteroid mining than I do in other topics, and this enabled me to be far more specific in the QFS, this higher level of knowledge (and the specificity it enables) is actually unnecessary. As long as the researcher has a layman's level of knowledge in a given topic, they can spring from the structure of the QFS into organized research.

In particular, the square proper and the latchkey obstacles, synergies, key players, and wildcards components are meant to inter-inform. In realizing a key player for the research industry/event, a researcher may have the desire to change the QFS to reflect this – and they should do so. While each part of the QFS and follow up are designed to probe your mind in different ways, they are one cohesive tool designed to best inform directions for future research.

The above discussion has been centered on the initial purpose behind the development of the Qualitative Futures Square. However, time and again I've mentioned how the QFS is actually an incredibly flexible tool, not only capable – but worthy of being used in a multitude of manners. So, without further delay, let's examine utilizing the QFS to lead group planning/brainstorming.

Chapter 4: Using the QFS to Lead Groups

If I'm half as capable of predicting the future as I believe myself to be, there's quite a number of you readers that became interested in the QFS for its described capacity to lead group discussions. As I would hate to disappoint you, this will be the first alternate usage explored. The Qualitative Futures Square is an incredibly flexible tool, useful for everything from leading brainstorming sessions, to goalsetting, to aggregating data and mapping projections.

The QFS is well suited to leading brainstorming sessions. As such, we'll utilize brainstorming as the primary example for this chapter (even though it is also useful by one's self). Qualitative Futures Square brainstorming sessions are effective in creating engagement as well as encouraging confidence, as the group guides the filling in of the square, they see the effectiveness of the method brought about by their own hand. By its nature of addressing multiple possible futures, it shifts from competitive to cooperative. In groups, many individuals like to see their own thoughts prevail. In the end, it's usually the thoughts of one person that end up dominating the discussion. Unfortunately, it's not necessarily the one with the best ideas, but rather the one with the greater force of personality. In addition, when confronted by said person with the greater force of personality, more intelligent but timid individuals will often knuckle under.

QFS led brainstorming can't necessarily prevent basic social tendencies. However, by having multiple, separate "right answers", the group as a whole is capable of contributing, even the more timid personalities. Furthermore, because there are multiple "right answers", even the more forceful personalities start to become cooperative once their main ideas are on the table.

With brainstorming, it is best to start with simple inputs into the individual plots. My standard method is to begin with the order discussed in the previous chapter. Starting from the right and filling left, on the first timeframe, which creates a base to operate from. Take note that you shouldn't ever consider individual data points in a QFS as cemented. Not even after the first development (it should truly stand as a living, breathing document), and certainly not during initial development – which is why I recommend an easily edited medium such as a whiteboard for in person brainstorming and a shared Google Doc on Drive for distance meetings.

After the initial completion of the first line, ask the group whether or not they're satisfied with the Order placement of each item, or whether it might be better to switch options around. In particular, ask about Probable vs

Possible. If there's indecision, make the switch and ask if that order is better than the first. Get the group comfortable with the idea that the QFS is *flexible*.

Now, analyze the data input so far into the square. Is there an option that fits into a separate order in the next timeframe? For example, if the Possible square is more similar to the Preferred square in the first timeline than the Probable, ask if the Possible outcome for the initial timeline will become the Probable outcome in the next timeline. If this is the case, you can utilize this to form a general pattern for the full QFS. While there are a number of reasons this may not work for a given QFS, a QFS square that starts with Possible/Preferred matched/most similar can generally continue the pattern of using the Possible data to fill the Probable for the next, with the Possible and Preferred once again matching. Furthermore, with QFS squares of this pattern, Probable and Poor generally match for a given timeframe. However, be careful. Ensure that each data point inherited from the previous timeframe actually belongs there, and you and the group aren't simply getting caught up in the pattern.

If there is much disagreement within the group, you may actually wish to ensure that the previously discussed pattern doesn't arise. Instead, developing a QFS with the outlying columns actually shifting which inner column they more resemble allows for a more uncertain future (which a higher level of disagreement within a knowledgeable group may indicate). There are many other reasons in which to having a shifting column pattern. The first timeframe may include a goal of the group being accomplished within the Preferred column. If this is the case, it should remain exclusively within the Preferred column. The Possible and Probable columns should reflect events outside of that goal. Now, if the group considers the goal being accomplished probable, then the Probable square for the next timeframe should reflect what would happen if that goal were accomplished – and if the group considers the accomplishment less likely, it should lie in the Possible column. If the group is not comfortable with it being the case for either the Probable or Possible columns for the next timeline, you may wish to reconsider said goal (and perhaps make it the goal for the next timeframe).

When using a process, no matter if a pattern arises, of inheriting data (which all QFS should use to at least some degree) in group sessions you should use visual aids to indicate inherited data. My personal method when leading groups using a whiteboard is to draw arrows pointing from the original data point to the inherited data point. This allows the group to have a clear visualization of the progression of events, and can help identify a pattern to the group. Once a pattern is made clear via visualization, this represents a point for the group to reflect. Is this pattern really reflective of what they believe will happen, or has this pattern simply become convenient? If Probable and Preferred are commonly matching up, is this wishful thinking? It may very well be that the current state is the most logical way forward, certainly don't dismiss that possibility. However, self-reflection is very important when attempting to foresee the future.

Try not to be too particular about any given data point within the QFS. Remember that the Qualitative Futures Square is designed to be a living, breathing document. If you, as the group leader, disagree with how a QFS develops, take it upon yourself to watch for developments over time that agree with your method of thinking, and ask the group to revisit the QFS later. It may change to closer fit your personal projections, and it may not. Don't force a group led QFS to conform to your own thoughts (with extreme exceptions where the data is overwhelmingly in another direction, but if this is the case, you may wish to reconsider the members of the group). First and foremost, the QFS is designed to accommodate multiple possible paths.

Below is a group brainstormed Qualitative Futures Square developed during my time with Chiron Studies at Portland State University on space-based agriculture:

Space-based Agriculture	Poor	Possible	Probable	Preferred
Short Range (<5 years)	Crops not yet on board the ISS.	Crops are growing aboard the ISS.	Crops not yet on board the ISS.	Crops are growing aboard the ISS.
Middle Range (5-20 years)	Crops are growing, but only for research.	Crops are feeding the crew of the ISS.	Crops are partially feeding the crew of the ISS.	Crops are completely feeding the crew of the ISS.
Long Range (20-50 years)	Crops are feeding the crew of the ISS.	Crops are feeding an off-world colony.	Crops are feeding the crew of the ISS.	Crops are feeding an off-world colony.
Beyond (50-100 years)	Not yet an off-world colony to feed.	Not yet an off-world colony to feed.	Crops are feeding an off-world colony.	Crops are feeding multiple off-world colonies.

As you can see, this Qualitative Futures Square closely matches the first pattern discussed earlier. Aside from the Beyond timeframe, which the group considered to only hinge upon the status of off-world colonies, for growing crops to feed the crew of the ISS will actually be a harder engineering challenge than to grow crops on an off-world settlement (microgravity being rather difficult). By looking at the QFS, you can see that the group considers the major challenges of space-based agriculture being solved as a possibility within 20 years, and as a probability within 50.

One thing to think about is that I, as the only person actually knowledgeable about space exploration in the group, played only a very minor part (the Preferred outcome for Beyond was my creation) in filling the data points. Despite the average member's lack of knowledge on space exploration, what resulted is a fairly reasonable brainstorming QFS. While there's not the same amount of input in each square as there was in the asteroid mining QFS earlier, the accuracy was rather remarkable.

Chapter 5: Other QFS Uses

So far, we have covered two primary uses of the Qualitative Futures Square: futures hypotheses and brainstorming. The next usage to cover is goalsetting. Goalsetting with a QFS is useful for both individual goalsetting (such as for results from exercising/dieting) and group goalsetting (such as for team goals on the development timeframe for a piece of software).

Goalsetting is a change of pace for the Qualitative Futures Square. There's the most obvious way, in which goalsetting over the standard timelines is often not the most useful. While I may have goals in the Beyond standard timeframe, most people (and businesses) do not – and that's perfectly fine. There's another way in which goalsetting marks a change of pace, and that's deliberately creating a pattern for the data set. In this, it's best to make sure that the Preferred squares and the Probable squares are the most closely aligned, otherwise you may wish to reconsider your goals. In addition, while the relationship between Poor and Possible would also be closer than between either of them and the other two, they should not overlap as closely as Preferred and Probable. This is to allow for a "Plan B" type of goal, which is not mentally associated with failure (as Poor will inevitably be). By allowing for room between Possible and Poor, you create multiple pathways to success (even if the definition of success must be a tad flexible).

Returning to timeframes, the chosen definitions will of course depend entirely upon the goals being set. I won't go into a full blown explanation of the best practices of goalsetting, that's beyond the scope of this book. Some simple advice is to stay reasonable in so far as what can be accomplished. In particular in reference to Qualitative Futures Squares, determine when you can reasonable expect milestones, and build the timeframes around them. With goalsetting, you don't want a square to simply reflect "to still be in the process of X", you want a concrete outcome. The final change of pace is that each Order should be considered as slightly-interdependent, but separately evolving timelines. Meaning, for example, the Possible outcome for a non-initial timeframe should depend primarily upon the Possible outcome for the prior timeframe, and secondarily on the Probable outcome for the same timeframe. While you don't want to allow a project to get too far behind, it's important to acknowledge that it's difficult (though not impossible) to catch up once behind.

Goalsetting is a great point in which to introduce "tributary Qualitative Futures Squares" or tQFS. Say that you want to use a QFS for exercise goals. You start with the timeframes of

- <1 year
- 1-2 years
- 2-5 years
- 5-10 years

Starting from a point where one is not "fit", this is rather reasonable. Each timeframe should mark a milestone in being fit. While using a QFS means that you should acknowledge multiple possible futures, I'm going to address only Preferred within this paragraph, for the sake of simplicity. Within a year, you would like to have an average bodyweight for your height. Within two, you plan to be able to jog two miles without having to stop. Within five years, you would like to be capable of jogging five miles without rest. Before ten years have passed, you would like to run a marathon. These are all reasonable goals, and clear milestones. However, in order to help the chances of success, you may wish to also plan out milestones on the path to each of those milestones. To do so, you can use tQFS to plan out the insides of each timeframe, with four sub-timeframes. For example with <1 year:

- <3 months
- 3-6 months
- 6-9 months
- 9-12 months

For tQFS, I would always segment the sub-timeframes in equal duration as above. This both marks them as different from standard QFS and allows for smooth continuity between each tQFS. There are a few important things to keep in mind with tQFS. First, the final timeframe of tQFS should always be fully identical to the respective timeframe it's covering in the primary QFS. Second, in goalsetting, the continuity of separate timelines should continue across tQFS – the Probable outcomes in subsequent tQFS should progress naturally from the Probable outcomes in the prior tQFS, and so on. Third, you should have identical outcomes in each Order of the final Beyond timeframe, and instead the Preferred/Probable/Possible/Poor outcomes will be differentiated by having a more specific timeframe included to accomplish the final Beyond goal.

It's especially important to remember with goalsetting that the QFS (as well as tQFS) is designed to be a living, breathing document. If, within the timeframe of one tQFS you do fall behind, you don't need to stay in "Plan B" forever. Reformulate your subsequent tQFS (and primary QFS) based upon how things actually played out. Don't edit history and change your now completed tQFS, but it's actually important to now make your current trajectory the basis for the Probable trajectory into the future.

Let's move onto group goalsetting. Why would you use a QFS for team goalsetting in a professional environment? First and foremost, I'm not the first to argue for utilizing cooperative goalsetting with subordinates. The data shows that subordinates take mental ownership of goals they had a hand in creating, and are more motivated to accomplish them. Next is the dilemma that we're *not creating a solid timeline*. This may be an anathema to many managers, but for complex projects, this is really the best way forward. Consistent with the data in cooperative goalsetting, subordinates that have a hand in creating their goals using the QFS take mental ownership of the Preferred category and se0ek to accomplish those goals. In addition, as discussed earlier, it's often difficult to catch up once behind. Having clear goals in the event that you do fall behind is incredibly important. You may still want to accomplish the Probable/Preferred goals within the next timeframe, but having a Plan B allows a subordinate to have more autonomous capacity.

Of course, the amount of autonomy allowed (and the amount of input from the subordinate in the formulation process) will depend upon the relationship between yourself and the subordinate(s) in question. While I would advocate to err on the side of (slightly) too much autonomy, management styles differ. Just as best practices for goalsetting are outside the scope of this book, best practices for management are also outside the scope of this book. Regardless of your management style, this method of group goalsetting is useful for both working with a subordinate one-on-one and managing goals for a team equally.

In fact, this is where another method of segmenting QFS comes into play. When managing a team, there should be a main QFS that covers the entire project, and then a QFS for each team member. Each team member QFS should indicate in the final timeframe how the accomplishment of the final goals contributes to the overall team goals. tQFS may also be of use here. While the main project should remain consistently covered by one QFS, for longer term projects, team member QFS should be the ones segmented into tQFS.

Let's take a look at a QFS/tQFS set, using the earlier example of fitness:

Fitness Plan Main QFS	Poor	Possible	Probable	Preferred
Short Range (<1 year)	BMI 27 +/- 1	BMI 25 +/- 1	BMI 22 +/- 1	BMI 22
Middle Range (1-2 years)	Jog a mile with one stop	Jog a mile without stopping	Jogs two miles without stopping	Jogs two miles without stopping
Long Range (2-5 years)	Jogs two miles without stopping	Jog a mile every morning	Jog five miles without stopping	Jog five miles without stopping
Beyond (5-10 years)	Jog four miles without stopping	Jog five miles without stopping	Run a marathon	Finish first in a marathon

Fitness Plan Short Range tQFS	Poor	Possible	Probable	Preferred
<3 months	BMI 35	BMI 32 +/- 1	BMI 30 +/- 1	BMI 30
3-6 months	BMI 32 +/- 1	BMI 29 +/- 1	BMI 27 +/- 1	BMI 27
6-9 months	BMI 29 +/- 1	BMI 27 +/- 1	BMI 25 +/-1	BMI 25
9-12 months	BMI 27 +/- 1	BMI 25 +/- 1	BMI 22 +/- 1	BMI 22

Fitness Plan Mid-Range tQFS	Poor	Possible	Probable	Preferred
12-15 months	BMI 25 +/- 1	BMI 22 +/- 1	Jog a mile with two stops	Jog a mile with two stops
15-18 months	BMI 22 +/- 1	Jog a mile with two stops	Jog a mile with one stop	Jog a mile with one stop
18-21 months	Jog a mile with two stops	Jog a mile with one stop	Jog two miles with one stop	Jog two miles with one stop
21-24 months	Jog a mile with one stop	Jog a mile without stopping	Jog two miles without stopping	Jog two miles without stopping

Fitness Plan Long Range tQFS	Poor	Possible	Probable	Preferred
24-33 months	Jog a mile without stopping	Jog two miles without stopping	Jog three miles without stopping	Jog three miles without stopping
33-42 months	Jog two miles with two stops	Jog three miles with one stop	Jog a mile every morning	Jog a mile every morning
42-51 months	Jog two miles with one stop	Jog three miles without stopping	Jog four miles without stopping	Jog four miles without stopping
51-60 months	Jog two miles without stopping	Jog a mile every morning	Jog five miles without stopping	Jog five miles without stopping

Fitness Plan Beyond tQFS	Poor	Possible	Probable	Preferred
60-75 months	Jog three miles with one stop	Jog four miles without stopping	Jog a mile and a half every morning	Jog two miles every morning
75-90 months	Jog three miles without stopping	Jog five miles with two stops	Jog two miles every morning	Jog three miles every morning
90-105 months	Jog a mile every morning	Jog five miles with one stop	Jog three miles every morning	Run a marathon
105-120 months	Jog four miles without stopping	Jog five miles without stopping	Run a marathon	Finish first in a marathon

Chapter 6: Bringing it Home

So, you decided to give the Qualitative Futures Square a try for your hypothesis for a futures paper. You've done your research, accumulated your data, and have typed the main body of your technical document. It's time to write the executive summary, and you glance back at the Qualitative Futures Square. To be sure, it's far more concise than what is going to be a rather confusing set of paragraphs for an executive not used to reading along multiple, separately evolving timelines. Too bad you can't use it here. Or can you?

After all the talk in this book about the QFS being flexible, going that far may seem a tad condescending, but it's not meant to be whatsoever. The reason for this being, that that was actually my thought process at one point in time. Initially, the Qualitative Futures Square was going to be a private tool for my own benefit, one that I supplanted with roughly similar written paragraphs in a final document. As an unestablished tool of my own design, I had little confidence originally that anyone else would be interested in it. However, I was working on a project around the impact of technological unemployment, and I couldn't shake the feeling that the QFS was the best way to present my findings. So, I shot an email out asking if he was onboard for something a little unorthodox. He agreed, and his reaction when reading the QFS was gratifyingly positive. That one decision, and the encouragement that came from it, is what has led me onto the path to write this book.

So, my advice to the readers is: if you've examined the Qualitative Futures Square, found it useful for constructing a hypothesis, and agree (at least roughly) with most of what I've said about it, go for it – submit it as your executive summary.

There's little different in creating a QFS for a futures hypothesis and for an executive summary, other than keeping in mind that you're creating this for the benefit of someone likely without your technical education, rather than yourself as with the hypothesis – which is simply standard practice for constructing an executive summary anyway. The executive summary QFS will likely contain more information, but perhaps not be as technically in depth as the futures hypothesis QFS.

Not one to disappoint, below is first the futures hypothesis QFS that I first constructed for the technological unemployment project, and then the first executive summary QFS for the same topic:

Technological Unemployment	Poor	Possible	Probable	Preferred
Short Range (<5 years)	Basic data and office work may begin to be fully autonomous.	The newest wave of technological unemployment may not have hit yet.	Basic data and office work may begin to be fully autonomous.	The newest wave of technological unemployment may not have hit yet.
Middle Range (5-20 years)	Most data and office work may be autonomous. Transportation may begin to be autonomous.	Basic data and office work may begin to be mostly autonomous.	Most data and office work may be autonomous. Transportation may begin to be autonomous.	Basic data and office work may be complimented by smart software, not replaced.
Long Range (20-50 years)	Transportation may be mostly autonomous. Most manual labor may be autonomous.	About a quarter of the people may be left in each discussed job category from before, complimented by smart software.	Transportation may be mostly autonomous. Most manual labor may begin to be autonomous.	About half of the people may be left in each discussed job category from before, complimented by smart software.
Beyond (50-100 years)	Smart software and robotics may take over most jobs.	Jobs may be reduced to about twenty hours a week to allow more people to work, being complemented by robotics and smart software.	Smart software and robotics may take over half of current jobs.	New categories of jobs may be established to make room for unemployed workers. Even so, many jobs may be reduced in hours.

Latchkey issues: There aren't any real latchkey issues. Most of the above is based on logical progression from the current state, and isn't dependent upon make or break events.

Synergies: There are many areas of computer science which are synergistic with autonomous work, such as deep learning and other attempts to model intelligent behavior.

Key players: Alphabet is involved in multiple areas above, including autonomous transportation, smart software, and deep learning. There are many car companies that are also planning to implement autonomous behavior, notably Tesla vehicles being capable of autonomous behavior currently on private property.

Wildcards: The main wildcard is Artificial General Intelligence (AGI). AGI, being mentally equivalent to and/or greater than humans, can wildly change the projections within, depending on if/when such is achieved. The effect of this is incredibly hard to predict, and is often referred to as a "singularity" (entirely beyond the projectable horizon).

Executive summary version:

Technological Unemployment	Poor	Possible	Probable	Preferred
Short Range (<5 years)	Data entry, telemarketing, office work, and other clerical positions may begin to be fully autonomous. Transportation jobs may begin to be reduced.	Demand for clerical work may be reduced as workers are complimented by smart software.	Data entry, telemarketing, office work, and other clerical positions may begin to be fully autonomous.	Demand for clerical work may be slightly reduced as workers are complimented by smart software.
Middle Range (5-20 years)	Clerical work may be fully autonomous. Transportation and construction may be mostly autonomous.	Clerical work may be mostly autonomous. Interstate trucking may be largely autonomous.	Clerical work may be fully autonomous. Transportation and construction may be largely autonomous.	Demand for clerical workers may be about a quarter of current levels, being largely complimented by smart software.
Long Range (20-50 years)	Transportation and construction may be fully autonomous. Most restaurants may be fully automated. Smart software may reduce demand for engineers by half of current levels.	Clerical work, construction, and transportation may be mostly autonomous. Automated restaurants may be a more common novelty.	Transportation and construction may be fully autonomous. Fully automated restaurants may become common. Smart software may reduce demand for engineers.	Clerical work, construction, and transportation may be mostly autonomous. Automated restaurants may be a more common novelty.
Beyond (50-100 years)	Smart software and robotics may take over most jobs.	Jobs may be reduced to about twenty hours a week to allow more people to work, being complemented by robotics and smart software.	Smart software and robotics may take over half of current jobs.	New categories of jobs may be established to make room for unemployed workers. Even so, many jobs may be reduced in hours.

Latchkey issues: General public acceptance is latchkey for only a few categories of jobs, generally those that have a large component of customer service. While the ability to automate those jobs can easily be achieved, people may not wish to deal with automated customer service (as there is already some blowback for automated funneling systems for phone based customer service).

Synergies: There are many areas of computer science which are synergistic with autonomous work, such as deep learning and other attempts to model intelligent behavior. 3D printing is synergistic with fully autonomous construction, and can enable houses to be built at much faster rates. Electrical vehicle technology is synergistic with autonomous vehicles, where systems that allow electric based autonomous public transportation to run continuously, for far cheaper than current costs.

Key players: Alphabet (parent company of Google) is involved in multiple areas above, including autonomous transportation, smart software, and deep learning. They also have many longshot programs that could prove to be wildcard factors for the above, including the development of the below mentioned Artificial General Intelligence. Facebook, Amazon and Microsoft (each in separate areas) involved in these exact same areas. There are many car companies that are also planning/beginning to implement autonomous behavior, notably Tesla vehicles being capable of autonomous behavior currently on private property.

Wildcards: The main wildcard is Artificial General Intelligence (AGI). AGI, being mentally equivalent to and/or greater than humans, can wildly change the projections within, depending on if/when such is achieved. The effect of this is incredibly hard to predict, and is often referred to as a "singularity" (entirely beyond the projectable horizon).

Afterword

The Qualitative Futures Square is a powerful, flexible tool suited to many different uses. While I initially developed it as a method of generating concise futures hypotheses, through experimentation and usage it has become so much more. Every QFS shown in this book was developed elsewhere first, for an actual requested use (details of the fitness QFS have been changed though). The fact of the matter is, that I believe that I haven't even fully explored all of its uses.

As it stands, assuming you've read this whole book, you know roughly as much as I do about the theoretical usage of the QFS (sorry, I can't yet directly pass on my experience using it). I fully encourage you, the reader, to continue the process of innovation and explore alternate pathways to utilize the Qualitative Futures Square. I would be very interested in reading about new ways that readers have used the QFS, and I've included contact information in my author profile below.

The Qualitative Futures Square is of most use to those who are already experienced in futures studies, and passing on knowledge of the field itself is outside the scope of this book. However, for those interested, this book is the foundation for my series "Navigating the

Madness: Futures Studies". In addition, I will be transforming this book and all subsequent books in the series into courses on the Udemy platform. Updates for these will be available on my website and social media.

I hope that you've enjoyed reading this book as much as I enjoyed writing it. I sincerely hope that the information within this book will be useful to you, and that you'll use a Qualitative Futures Square at least once, if not on a regular basis. Let me know how much you enjoyed this work, what about the work you enjoyed, and whether or not you think you will use it.

Let's navigate the future together,

Adair Daniels

The Future is Coming

About the Author

Adair Daniels is a young US-based futurist, entrepreneur, and physics student focused on space-based potentials. As a futurist, he is the founder of Seize My Future – a website serving as a guide for those who wish to stay updated on the cutting edge of life. He has been published in The Future of Business with "Space-Based Solar Power and Wireless Power Transmission" and A Very Human Future with "Astro-mining for Abundancy". His overall futurism goals are to help the public understand the cutting edge of scientific and technological developments, while leading the charge to establish humanity as an interplanetary species.

As an entrepreneur, he is currently designing a personalized hub experience for every internet user. This hub will create a unique web for every person, connecting the internet in new and unique ways. It is seamlessly a platform for social media, news, blogs, and the rest of the internet. In the future, he hopes to get into the private space race by establishing a variety of space-based businesses. He also seeks to provide a way for the public to directly interact with space.

As a physics student at Portland State University, he is seeking to understand the most fundamental mysteries of the universe. Focusing on theoretical physics and cosmology, he hopes to help establish a unified theory of physics and to further study phenomena such as dark matter and black holes.

You can find him at:

http://www.adairdaniels.com

http://www.seizemyfuture.com

http://www.facebook.com/vesheeth

adairdaniels@gmail.com

Twitter: @AdairDaniels

www.ingramcontent.com/pod-product-compliance
Lightning Source LLC
Chambersburg PA
CBHW070338190526
45169CB00005B/1944